Bug in my brain

Copyright © 2015 by Audrey Eggers Thompson. All rights reserved.

No part of this publication may be reproduced, stored in a retrieval system or transmitted in any way by any means, electronic, mechanical, photocopy, recording or otherwise without the prior permission of the author except as provided by USA copyright law.

Printed in the United States of America. For bulk orders, contact publisher.

ISBN-13: 978-0692594858
ISBN-10: 069259485X

Write Way Publishing Company, LLC
WriteWayPublishingCompany.com

Dedication

This book is dedicated with love to
Evy, Cakes, John Mark, and supportive parents.

Acknowledgments

I would not have written the Gigi stories without my wonderful family. My daughters Evy and Cakes inspire me by showing the special love between a mom and her children every day. My husband John Mark Thompson provides encouragement and is patient with the (usually) mild chaos that surrounds me, and my parents always have given me their support for my dreams.

I also send warm thanks to my 2014 two-year-old class at Parkway Presbyterian Preschool for pretending to saw open my head (with fake tools thankfully) to find the bug in my brain; to Rosemary Luttrell, a very special editor and mother of one of my Parkway two-year-olds, because she encouraged me to publish my stories; to Gwenda Sonneveld who created the amazing illustrations for this book, and to Lee Heinrich at Write Way Publishing Company for being so awesome through publishing process! And last but not least I thank God for blessing my life so richly.

Bug in My Brain

One day I felt a wiggle in my brain, it made me giggle.

I asked my mom what it could be.

Maybe it's a bug, Gigi!

Oh, Gigi darling, your brain's too happy

O silly girl, it could not be

a stingy, grumpy bumblebee.

Oh, Mom, I know! I'm going to chant!

Philly is an ANT! ANT! ANT!

Oh no! An ant is far too small
to occupy your brain at all.

So, Gigi doll, you see it's true,
a little pipsqueak ant won't do!

Philly's got to be a cricket.

This idea, I just can't kick it.

But, Gigi, crickets sing and chirp

That would mean your brain would burp!

Oh no, Gigi, I don't buy it. Okay now please let me try it.

No other bug can compete.

So you see, Gigi my dear,
it has now become quite clear

that brain bug Philly you should not fear.

In fact, he's flying out your ear!

Come on, Gigi, let's say goodbye.
FLY HIGH SWEET BUTTERFLY!!!

Audrey Eggers Thompson: *Author*

Audrey has worked with kids, one way or another, most of her life, including formerly as owner and operator of Bizi Kidz Drop-In Child Care in Winston-Salem, NC and presently as a pre-school teacher, a job she loves. Her motto has always been "the more the merrier" and that pertains to children, family, animals, and friends. Which is a good thing since she is mom to two delightful daughters, two dogs, one cat, various other animals from time to time, and wife to the wonderful John Mark. Born in Mobile, Alabama in 1982, Audrey has lived most of her life in beautiful Winston-Salem, NC.

Her recent story-telling skills surprised everyone, including Audrey, when one day out of the clear blue, she said her brain started thinking up rhyming stories about a little girl named Gigi, and a series developed loosely based on her experiences with her own children, so now Audrey is an author! Fittingly, her first book is *Bug in My Brain*.

Gwenda Sonneveld: *Illustrator*

Dutch illustrator, designer, and photographer Gwenda Sonneveld studied visualizing at Graphic Lyceum Rotterdam and has since worked on many illustration projects. She spent a wonderful year traveling around Europe absorbing the sights, colors, and culture. She is currently living in Dublin, Ireland and loves her job as a freelance children's book illustrator. She enjoys the theater, music festivals, sculpting, languages (she speaks several!), and animals and admits to a fondness for games and PlayStation in her spare time.

Made in the USA
Middletown, DE
15 December 2015